More Lists!

The Fill-It-In, Pass-It-Around Book for You and Your Friends

I can cross my eyes.

My favorite color is neon green.

I've tried sushi—it was good!

illustrated by
Angela Martini

Published by American Girl Publishing
Copyright © 2012 by American Girl

Questions or comments? Call 1-800-845-0005,
visit **americangirl.com**, or write to Customer Service,
American Girl, 8400 Fairway Place, Middleton, WI 53562-0497.

Printed in China
12 13 14 15 16 17 LEO 10 9 8 7 6 5 4 3 2 1

Editorial Development: Mary Richards Beaumont
Art Direction and Design: Lisa Wilber
Production: Tami Kepler, Sarah Boecher,
Jeannette Bailey, Judith Lary

Illustrations: Angela Martini

Dear Reader,

Sure, you know your friends and family. But do you know
their favorite cookie flavors? Or how many of them can
tap dance? Or who among everyone you know has had
stitches? This book is jam-packed with questions and
activities to help you find out.

You'll learn loads of things you never knew about the
people in your life—some hilarious, some surprising,
some completely amazing. You can expect hours of
"Wow!" and "I didn't know that!" as you complete your
book of lists. You and your friends can use the included
stickers to comment on others' entries. And when you're
finished, you'll have a book that's completely unique—
just like you.

All you have to do is grab a pencil and write on!

Your friends at American Girl

Everybody's Favorites

Invite your friends or family to fill in their favorites, or use the topics as icebreaker questions at your next party. Don't forget to add your own favorites!

My favorite song

Name: Song title:

-------------------------------   -------------------------------

-------------------------------   -------------------------------

-------------------------------   -------------------------------

-------------------------------   -------------------------------

-------------------------------   -------------------------------

-------------------------------   -------------------------------

-------------------------------   -------------------------------

-------------------------------   -------------------------------

-------------------------------   -------------------------------

-------------------------------   -------------------------------

-------------------------------   -------------------------------

-------------------------------   -------------------------------

My favorite ice cream flavor

Name: Flavor:

-----------------------------------   -----------------------------------

-----------------------------------   -----------------------------------

-----------------------------------   -----------------------------------

-----------------------------------   -----------------------------------

-----------------------------------   -----------------------------------

-----------------------------------   -----------------------------------

-----------------------------------   -----------------------------------

-----------------------------------   -----------------------------------

-----------------------------------   -----------------------------------

-----------------------------------   -----------------------------------

-----------------------------------   -----------------------------------

-----------------------------------   -----------------------------------

Draw it!

My favorite shoes

Name: ------------------------

Name: ------------------------

Name: ------------------------

Name: ------------------------

Name: ------------------------

Name: ------------------------

My favorite book

Name:

Book title:

My favorite color

Name:

Color:

My favorite snack

Name:

Snack:

-------------------------------- --------------------------------

-------------------------------- --------------------------------

-------------------------------- --------------------------------

-------------------------------- --------------------------------

-------------------------------- --------------------------------

-------------------------------- --------------------------------

-------------------------------- --------------------------------

-------------------------------- --------------------------------

-------------------------------- --------------------------------

-------------------------------- --------------------------------

-------------------------------- --------------------------------

-------------------------------- --------------------------------

My favorite movie

Name:

Movie title:

_____

_____

_____

_____

_____

_____

_____

_____

_____

_____

_____

_____

Draw it!

My favorite carnival ride

Name: _____   Name: _____

Name: _____   Name: _____

Name: _____   Name: _____

My favorite cookie

Name:

Cookie:

My favorite TV show

Name:

TV show title:

My favorite animal

Name:

Animal:

My favorite breakfast cereal

Name: Cereal:

------------------------------   ------------------------------

------------------------------   ------------------------------

------------------------------   ------------------------------

------------------------------   ------------------------------

------------------------------   ------------------------------

------------------------------   ------------------------------

------------------------------   ------------------------------

------------------------------   ------------------------------

------------------------------   ------------------------------

------------------------------   ------------------------------

------------------------------   ------------------------------

My favorite sports team

Name:

Team name:

My favorite candy

Name:

Candy:

My favorite thing to draw

Name: _____   Name: _____

Name: _____   Name: _____

Name: _____   Name: _____

My favorite pizza topping

Name:

Topping:

My favorite school subject

Name:

Subject:

My favorite cartoon character

Name:

Character name:

Family Facts

Find out lots about your family at your next reunion or holiday party! Ask the questions and fill in the answers yourself, or pass the book around to different adult relatives and ask them to write in answers about what they were like when they were your age. If someone lives far away, you could even mail the book to that person to complete.

Name: --

Your favorite toy when you were little: ---------------------------

----

Your nicknames: --

What pets did you have? (Don't forget their names!) -----------------

----

Your least-favorite chore: --

Your best school subject: ---

Your first job: ---

What you wanted to be when you grew up: ---------------------------

----

Your proudest moment: ---

Advice you'd give to your kid self: -------------------------------

----

Name: --

Your favorite toy when you were little: ---------------------------------

----

Your nicknames: ---

What pets did you have? (Don't forget their names!) ---------------------

----

Your least-favorite chore: --

Your best school subject: ---

Your first job: ---

What you wanted to be when you grew up: ---------------------------------

----

Your proudest moment: --

Advice you'd give to your kid self: ---------------------------------------

----

Name: _____

Your favorite toy when you were little: _____

_____

Your nicknames: _____

_____

What pets did you have? (Don't forget their names!) _____

_____

_____

Your least-favorite chore: _____

Your best school subject: _____

Your first job: _____

What you wanted to be when you grew up: _____

_____

Your proudest moment: _____

_____

Advice you'd give to your kid self: _____

_____

Name: _____

Your favorite toy when you were little: _____

_____

Your nicknames: _____

_____

What pets did you have? (Don't forget their names!) _____

_____

_____

Your least-favorite chore: _____

Your best school subject: _____

Your first job: _____

What you wanted to be when you grew up: _____

_____

Your proudest moment: _____

_____

Advice you'd give to your kid self: _____

_____

Name: _____

Your favorite toy when you were little: _____

_____

Your nicknames: _____

_____

What pets did you have? (Don't forget their names!) _____

_____

_____

Your least-favorite chore: _____

Your best school subject: _____

Your first job: _____

What you wanted to be when you grew up: _____

_____

Your proudest moment: _____

_____

Advice you'd give to your kid self: _____

_____

Name: --

Your favorite toy when you were little: ----------------

Your nicknames: --------------------------------

What pets did you have? (Don't forget their names!) ----------------

----

Your least-favorite chore: --------------------------

Your best school subject: --------------------------

Your first job: ----------------------------------

What you wanted to be when you grew up: ----------------

Your proudest moment: ----------------------------

Advice you'd give to your kid self: --------------------

Out of Order?

Do you have the personality of a child born first, last, or somewhere in between? Take this quiz to find out—and ask your friends to try it, too!

1. Which of these gift coupons would you give to a parent as a gift?
   a. Good for one day of help around the house
   b. Good for one evening of free babysitting
   c. Good for settling one argument between your siblings
   d. Good for ten hugs and kisses

2. Whew! You just printed out a five-page report for school. What do you do next?
   a. Hope the teacher likes it so much that she asks you to read it to the class.
   b. Check for mistakes, find one, and reprint the whole report.
   c. Give yourself a pat on the back for getting it done on time, and go call one of your friends.
   d. Make a beautiful cover for it.

3. Today is your birthday! You've planned the party activities, but your guests start to play another game instead. What do you say?
   a. "It's my birthday, so I get to pick what we do."
   b. "But this is a tropical-themed party, and that's not a tropical game."
   c. "Fun! I love that game."
   d. "If you think that game is good, wait 'til you see what we're going to do now!"

4. Fast-forward to the year 2042. Where are you?
    a. Being interviewed about what it was like to take a solo cross-country bicycle trip
    b. Working on making the world a better place from your desk in the White House
    c. Being a family counselor, helping people solve their problems and get along better
    d. Starting your own business writing and illustrating funny children's books

5. Hooray for the weekend! What is your favorite way to spend time on Saturday?
    a. Shopping with Mom and then curling up with a good book
    b. Tackling a challenging craft project
    c. Getting a bunch of friends together for a movie marathon
    d. Hanging around doing whatever the rest of the family is doing

Turn the page to see if your answers match your place in your family.

Answers

Here's what some experts say about your answers. See if you agree. Then ask other members of your family to take the quiz, too!

Mostly a's

You're like an outstanding only child. Confident and mature, you like getting attention. You're good at spending time alone, and you believe you can do just about anything without help.

That's me: _____

_____

_____

_____

Mostly b's

You're like a fabulous firstborn. You're responsible and organized, and you try to do things just right. Pleasing adults is important to you, and your natural leadership skills shine, no matter whom you're with.

That's me: _____

_____

_____

_____

Mostly c's

You're like a marvelous middle child. Getting along with people is easy for you. When things don't exactly go your way, you're easy-going, but you know how to compromise to get what you want.

That's me: _____

_____

_____

_____

Mostly d's

You're like the brilliant baby of the family. Creativity, friendliness, and a great sense of humor are a few of your strong points. You try lots of new things because you're not afraid to fail.

That's me: _____

_____

_____

_____

Have You Ever . . . ?

Find out all kinds of crazy stuff about your friends
and family! The first person to mark each statement
as true about himself or herself can tell more of
the story. Anyone else who can also claim
that it's true can fill in his or her name.

I have traveled to another country.

Name: _____

Where: _____

What I did: _____

_____

Me, too!

_____   _____
Name   Name

_____   _____
Name   Name

_____   _____
Name   Name

I've ridden in a hot-air balloon.

Name: _____

Where: _____

_____

Me, too!

_____   _____
Name   Name

_____   _____
Name   Name

_____   _____
Name   Name

I've eaten sushi.

Name: _____

What kind: _____

_____

Me, too!

_____   _____
Name   Name

_____   _____
Name   Name

_____   _____
Name   Name

I've eaten pizza with anchovies.

Name: _____

Where: _____

_____

Me, too!

_____   _____
Name   Name

_____   _____
Name   Name

_____   _____
Name   Name

I have met a celebrity.

Name: _____

Who: _____

Where: _____

Me, too!

---------------------------------   ---------------------------------
         Name   Name

---------------------------------   ---------------------------------
         Name   Name

---------------------------------   ---------------------------------
         Name   Name

I've petted an exotic animal.

Name: _____

What kind: _____

Where: _____

Me, too!

---------------------------------   ---------------------------------
         Name   Name

---------------------------------   ---------------------------------
         Name   Name

---------------------------------   ---------------------------------
         Name   Name

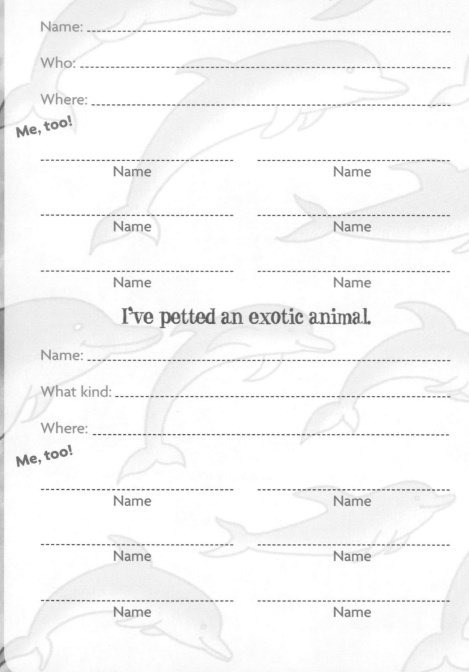

I've gone snorkeling.

Name: _____

Where: _____

One thing I saw: _____

_____

Me, too!

_____   _____
          Name   Name

_____   _____
          Name   Name

_____   _____
          Name   Name

I've swum with dolphins.

Name: _____

Where: _____

_____

Me, too!

_____   _____
          Name   Name

_____   _____
          Name   Name

_____   _____
          Name   Name

I've been to a professional ballgame.

Name: --

Who played: --

Me, too!

Name   Name

Name   Name

Name   Name

I've hugged a mascot.

Name: --

Which one: --

Me, too!

Name   Name

Name   Name

Name   Name

I've performed in front of more than 1,000 people at a time.

Name: _____

What I did: _____

_____

Me, too!

_____   _____
Name   Name

_____   _____
Name   Name

_____   _____
Name   Name

I've acted in a play.

Name: _____

My character: _____

Me, too!

_____   _____
Name   Name

_____   _____
Name   Name

_____   _____
Name   Name

I've ridden a horse.

Name: ....

Where: ....

Its name: ....

Me, too!

-------------------------------------   -------------------------------------
          Name   Name

-------------------------------------   -------------------------------------
          Name   Name

-------------------------------------   -------------------------------------
          Name   Name

I've been on TV.

Name: ....

Here's why: ....

....

Me, too!

-------------------------------------   -------------------------------------
          Name   Name

-------------------------------------   -------------------------------------
          Name   Name

-------------------------------------   -------------------------------------
          Name   Name

I can tap-dance.

Name: --

A song I've tap-danced to: --

Me, too!

-- --
Name   Name

-- --
Name   Name

-- --
Name   Name

I can do an impression of someone else.

Name: --

Who I can impersonate: --

Me, too!

-- --
Name   Name

-- --
Name   Name

-- --
Name   Name

I've won a contest.

Name: --

What I won: ---

Me, too!

--   --
Name   Name

--   --
Name   Name

--   --
Name   Name

I've eaten an entire banana split.

Name: --

Its flavors: ---

Me, too!

--   --
Name   Name

--   --
Name   Name

--   --
Name   Name

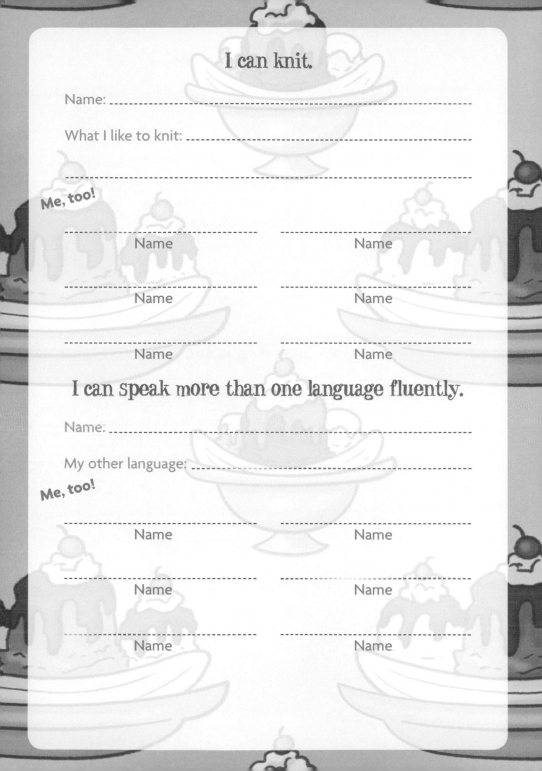

I can knit.

Name: ....

What I like to knit: ....

....

Me, too!

---------------------------------- ----------------------------------
Name   Name

---------------------------------- ----------------------------------
Name   Name

---------------------------------- ----------------------------------
Name   Name

I can speak more than one language fluently.

Name: ....

My other language: ....

Me, too!

---------------------------------- ----------------------------------
Name   Name

---------------------------------- ----------------------------------
Name   Name

---------------------------------- ----------------------------------
Name   Name

I've won a spelling bee.

Name: _____

My winning word: _____

Me, too!

-----------------------------	-----------------------------
Name	Name
-----------------------------	-----------------------------
Name	Name
-----------------------------	-----------------------------
Name	Name

I've broken a bone.

Name: _____

My broken bone: _____

How it happened: _____

_____

Me, too!

-----------------------------	-----------------------------
Name	Name
-----------------------------	-----------------------------
Name	Name
-----------------------------	-----------------------------
Name	Name

I've had stitches.

Name: --

Where: --

For what: --

Me, too!

------------------------------------   ------------------------------------
Name   Name

------------------------------------   ------------------------------------
Name   Name

------------------------------------   ------------------------------------
Name   Name

I've been elected.

Name: --

The job: --

Me, too!

------------------------------------   ------------------------------------
Name   Name

------------------------------------   ------------------------------------
Name   Name

------------------------------------   ------------------------------------
Name   Name

I can bake a treat from scratch.

Name: _____

My favorite thing to bake: _____

_____

Me, too!

------------------------------ ------------------------------
Name   Name

------------------------------ ------------------------------
Name   Name

------------------------------ ------------------------------
Name   Name

I can cook something without a recipe.

Name: _____

What it is: _____

Me, too!

------------------------------ ------------------------------
Name   Name

------------------------------ ------------------------------
Name   Name

------------------------------ ------------------------------
Name   Name

I've trained an animal to do a trick.

Name: _____

The animal: _____

The trick: _____

Me, too!

_____   _____
Name   Name

_____   _____
Name   Name

_____   _____
Name   Name

I have been in a parade.

Name: _____

With this group: _____

Me, too!

_____   _____
Name   Name

_____   _____
Name   Name

_____   _____
Name   Name

I've sung a solo.

Name: ....

Where: ....

The song: ....

Me, too!

....
Name   Name

....
Name   Name

....
Name   Name

I can whistle.

Name: ....

My favorite song to whistle: ....

....

Me, too!

....
Name   Name

....
Name   Name

....
Name   Name

I can snowboard.

Name: _____

Here's a trick I can do: _____

_____

Me, too!

_____   _____
Name   Name

_____   _____
Name   Name

_____   _____
Name   Name

I can hit a baseball or softball.

Name: _____

My favorite baseball or softball player: _____

_____

Me, too!

_____   _____
Name   Name

_____   _____
Name   Name

_____   _____
Name   Name

I've been lost.

Name: _____

Where: _____

How I was found: _____

_____

Me, too!

| _____ | _____ |
| Name | Name |

| _____ | _____ |
| Name | Name |

| _____ | _____ |
| Name | Name |

I've rescued something.

Name: _____

What: _____

Me, too!

| _____ | _____ |
| Name | Name |

| _____ | _____ |
| Name | Name |

| _____ | _____ |
| Name | Name |

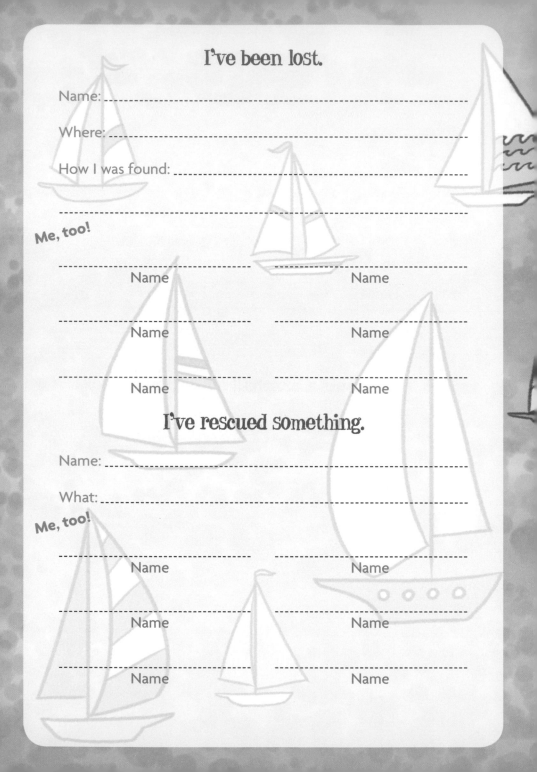

I can water-ski.

Name: _____

A sketch of my favorite swimsuit:

Me, too!

_____ Name	_____ Name
_____ Name	_____ Name
_____ Name	_____ Name

I've been on a sailboat.

Name: _____

The boat's name: _____

Me, too!

_____ Name	_____ Name
_____ Name	_____ Name
_____ Name	_____ Name

I can do a magic trick.

Name: ....

The trick: ....

Me, too!

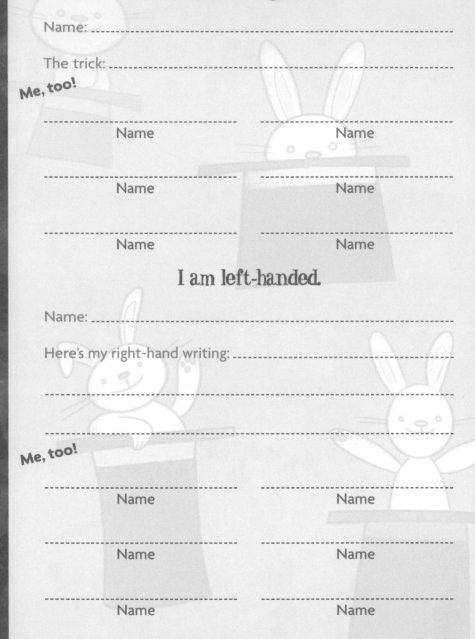

------------------------------------- | -------------------------------------
Name | Name

------------------------------------- | -------------------------------------
Name | Name

------------------------------------- | -------------------------------------
Name | Name

I am left-handed.

Name: ....

Here's my right-hand writing: ....

....

....

Me, too!

------------------------------------- | -------------------------------------
Name | Name

------------------------------------- | -------------------------------------
Name | Name

------------------------------------- | -------------------------------------
Name | Name

I've been to the top of a skyscraper.

Name: --

Where: ---

What I saw: ---

Me, too!

Name

Name

Name

Name

Name

Name

I've read an entire chapter book in one day.

Name: --

The book: --

How I felt when I finished: ---

Me, too!

Name

Name

Name

Name

Name

Name

Do You Dare?

How adventurous are you? For each activity, circle how likely you would be to try it. Ask your friends to try this quiz, too!

Explore a cave

I'd love it!   I might try it.   Count me out!

Climb a volcano

I'd love it!   I might try it.   Count me out!

Introduce yourself to a person who speaks a different language

I'd love it!   I might try it.   Count me out!

Ask someone famous for her or his autograph

I'd love it!   I might try it.   Count me out!

Audition for a musical

I'd love it!   I might try it.   Count me out!

Try an unfamiliar type of food

I'd love it!   I might try it.   Count me out!

Go white-water rafting

I'd love it!   I might try it.   Count me out!

Swing on a trapeze

I'd love it!   I might try it.   Count me out!

Spend a year on a boat

I'd love it!   I might try it.   Count me out!

Hold an iguana

I'd love it!   I might try it.   Count me out!

Camp in a forest without a tent

I'd love it!   I might try it.   Count me out!

Swim in a deep lake

I'd love it!   I might try it.   Count me out!

Results

Mostly "I'd love it!"

You don't think twice about doing new and different things. You figure that you won't know if you like something until you try it.

That's me: ....

....

....

Mostly "I might try it."

You dare with care. You like to ask questions and think about the risks before taking the plunge.

That's me: ....

....

....

Mostly "Count me out!"

You go with what you know and do what feels comfortable. Just remember that doing something new can be fun, too!

That's me: ....

....

....

Friendship Challenges

You and a friend can learn a lot about each other by just doing stuff together. Pick a friend, and try a challenge. Write down what you did when you're done—and what fun things you learned in the process.

Plant something.

☐ **Completed!**

What we did: --

What we learned: --

Make a craft.

☐ **Completed!**

What we did: --

What we learned: --

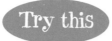

How to Make a Creative Container

Make this cute cup—and then use it to store your art and craft supplies. Attach one end of a long piece of ribbon to the top edge of a sturdy box with a Glue Dot. Tightly and neatly wrap the ribbon around the box, overlapping it slightly. Secure with more Glue Dots around the way. When you get to the bottom of the box, trim the ribbon and attach the end with another Glue Dot.

Optional: Add a contrasting ribbon on top of the first layer.

Bake something with ingredients you both like.

☐ Completed!

What we did: ....

....

What we learned: ....

....

Help someone.

☐ Completed!

What we did: ....

....

What we learned: ....

....

Write a rhyming poem.

What we did: _____

_____

What we learned: _____

_____

Jump rope 100 times without messing up.

What we did: _____

_____

What we learned: _____

_____

Give each other wacky hairstyles.

☐ Completed!

What we did: --

What we learned: --

Give each other pretty hairstyles.

☐ Completed!

What we did: --

What we learned: --

How to Do a Cute Braided 'Do

It's a simple style with a twist.

1. Part hair on the side. Separate a section of hair near your hairline from the rest of your hair. Use an elastic to tie the rest of your hair into a ponytail. At the part, divide the sectioned hair into 3 equal parts.

2. Begin to braid, and add a small piece of hair from your hairline with each cross. When you reach the back of your head, secure braid with elastic.

3. Remove the elastic from your ponytail. Gather the braid into your ponytail, and re-tie the ponytail with the elastic. You can remove the elastic from the braid, or leave it in to make it more secure.

4. Finished! If you'd like, add a cute clip to decorate your braid.

Draw self-portraits.

Design a greeting card.

☐ Completed!

What we did: _____

_____

What we learned: _____

_____

Try a new food.

☐ Completed!

What we did: _____

_____

What we learned: _____

_____

Watch a black-and-white movie.

☐ Completed!

What we did: _____

_____

What we learned: _____

_____

Make up a dance.

☐ Completed!

What we did: --

What we learned: ---

Make up a joke.

☐ Completed!

What we did: --

What we learned: ---

How to Write a Joke (That's Actually Funny!)

1. Choose a noun, like an animal name—try "chimpanzee." It helps to pick a word that's already a little bit funny.

2. Look closely at the last sound in the word, and think of another word that starts with that sound. "Chimpanzee" ends with the sound "zee." So what's a word that starts with the same sound? "Zebra!" Mix the two words together to create your punch-line word. You'll end up with something like "Chimpanzebra."

3. To make up a question, think about the two words in your punch-line word. Make sure the question doesn't actually use those two words. Your question could include qualities from each animal. For example, a zebra is striped and fast, and a chimpanzee likes bananas.

4. Put your question and your punch line together:
Q: What's black and white, runs fast, and loves to eat bananas?
A: A chimpanzebra!

Ta-da!

Pal Poll

Ask a group of friends these questions.
The answers might surprise everyone!

Who here . . .

can cross her eyes?

Names: _____

_____

_____

has met one of her great-grandparents?

Names: _____

_____

_____

has lived in one house her whole life?

Names (and where): _____

_____

_____

has a big collection of something?

Names (and of what): _____

_____

_____

Who here . . .

is wearing colorful socks?

Names: --

----

can shoot a basket?

Names: --

----

has had a pet that's not a cat or dog?

Names (and what kind): ---

----

almost always wears jeans?

Names: --

Who here . . .

wears glasses?

Names: ....

....

....

has blue eyes?

Names: ....

....

....

can paint her own fingernails?

Names: ....

....

....

has seen an ocean?

Names (and where): ....

....

....

Who here . . .

can do the splits?

Names: --

----

has been on a roller coaster?

Names (and where): --

----

can curl her tongue?

Names: --

----

is afraid of spiders?

Names: --

Who here . . .

can recite a whole poem?

Names (and poem): --

----

can sing in front of a crowd?

Names: --

----

has curly hair?

Names: --

----

has braces?

Names: --

Who here . . .

has won an animal from a claw machine?

Names: --

----

believes in the three-second rule?

Names: --

----

can blow a bubble?

Names: --

----

can wrap a present perfectly?

Names: --

Who here . . .

has a good-luck charm?

Names (and what it is): ---

----

has had a tooth pulled?

Names: ---

----

likes snakes?

Names: ---

----

is superstitious?

Names (and of what): ---

Who here . . .

can play an instrument?

Names (and which one): ---

----

makes her bed every day?

Names: --

----

can break an egg neatly?

Names: --

----

has been in a wedding?

Names: --

Who here . . .

has an interesting scar?

Names (and where): _____

_____

_____

bites her fingernails?

Names: _____

_____

_____

can do a cartwheel?

Names: _____

_____

_____

remembers her dreams?

Names: _____

_____

_____

Name Game

Ask friends and family members for their answers to these questions—to come up with their new "names"!

Rodeo Champ

Your favorite Western state
+
The name of something you'd find on a mountain
=
Your rodeo name: **Montana Frost**

Name:

Rodeo name:

Super Spy

Something you'd find in a haunted house
$+$
The last name of your favorite teacher
$=$
Your spy name: **Shadow McGuthrie**

Name:	Spy name:

Fabulous Fairy

The name of a flower or plant
+
Something found in the sky
+
Fire
=
Your fairy name: **Willow Saturnfire**

Name:

Fairy name:

Sports Star

Your favorite team's mascot
+
The last name of your favorite sports star
=
Your sports name: **Wildcat Williams**

Name:

Sports star name:

Cartoon Character

Your first pet's name
+
Your favorite crayon color
=
Your cartoon character name: **Punky Indigo**

Name:	Cartoon character name:

Perfectly Pirate

A word that describes your favorite chips
+
An animal in the ocean
=
Your pirate name: **Crunchy Seahorse**

Name:

Pirate name:

Heroic Hero

The word "The"
+
Your birthstone
+
An insect that scares you
=
Your superhero name:
The Garnet Centipede

Name:

Superhero name:

Guess Who!

Play this fun game with a group. Punch out the game pieces, and pass one to each person, along with a pencil. Ask people to fill in something true about themselves that most people might not know about them.

Throw the slips into a hat, and pick out one at a time. Read the fact to the group, and see if anyone can guess whose it is. This works great for people who are getting to know one another as well as for parties of close friends!

a little-known fact
about me

a little-known fact
about me

a little-known fact
about me

a little-known fact
about me

a little-known fact
about me

a little-known fact
about me

a little-known fact
about me

a little-known fact
about me

a little-known fact
about me

a little-known fact
about me

a little-known fact
about me

a little-known fact
about me

a little-known fact
about me

a little-known fact
about me

a little-known fact
about me

a little-known fact
about me

a little-known fact
about me

a little-known fact
about me

a little-known fact
about me

a little-known fact
about me

a little-known fact
about me

a little-known fact
about me

a little-known fact
about me

a little-known fact
about me

Have you ever ...

filled out a list book?

Name: ....

had an idea for a funny list?

Name: ....

Idea: ....

Send your ideas to:

More Lists! Editor
American Girl
8400 Fairway Place
Middleton, WI 53562

(All comments and suggestions received by American Girl may be used without compensation or acknowledgment. Sorry, but photos can't be returned.)

Here are some other American Girl books you might like:

☐ I read it.

☐ I read it.

☐ I read it.

☐ I read it.

☐ I read it.

Stickers

Use these comment stickers to tag your friends' entries!

Awesome   Ha-Ha   Amazing!   Cute

SUPER COOL   Oh, no!   For real?   WOW

THE BEST EVER   WHAT?!?   Awesome   Ha-Ha

Amazing!   SUPER COOL   Oh, no!

Cute   For real?   WOW   Amazing!

WHAT?!?   THE BEST EVER   For real?   SUPER COOL

Awesome   Ha-Ha   WOW   Cute

Cute   Oh, no!   WHAT?!?

THE BEST EVER

Ha-Ha   SUPER COOL   For real?   Awesome